The Hard Shapes of Paradise

Alabama Poetry Series

GENERAL EDITORS: Chase Twichell and Thomas Rabbitt

In the Fourth World, by Sandra M. Gilbert
The Story They Told Us of Light, by Rodney Jones
The Middle of the Journey, by Brian Swann
Memling's Veil, by Mary Ruefle
Fields of Vision, by Mariève Rugo
A Belfry of Knees, by Alberta Turner
The Arctic Herd, by John Morgan
The Invention of Kindness, by Lee Upton
Any Given Day, by Ralph Burns
Esperanza's Hair, by Peggy Shumaker
Measure, by Thomas Swiss
Boy in a Boat, by Roy Bentley
Worlds Apart, by Richard Jackson
Life Without Speaking, by Mary Ruefle
The Hard Shapes of Paradise, by Paul Nelson
Voices in the House, by Susan Snively

PAUL NELSON

The Hard Shapes
of Paradise

The University of Alabama Press
Tuscaloosa and London

Library of Congress Cataloging-in-Publication Data

Nelson, Paul, 1934–
   The hard shapes of paradise.

   I. Title.
PS3564.E474H37   1988   811'.54   87-19221
ISBN 0-8173-0391-X (alk. paper)
ISBN 0-8173-0392-8 (pbk.)

British Library Cataloguing-in-Publication Data is available.

For Myrna Aidlin

Acknowledgments

My special gratitude to poet and critic Lorrie Goldensohn for her fine eye and willing temper.

Some of the poems in this collection appeared originally in the following journals:

Black Warrior Review
   "Benediction"
   "The Invention of Handball"

Calliope
   "Farmer"

Chairoscuro
   "The Difference"
   "Thaw"

Colorado Review
   "The Nature of Prayer"
   "Fathoms"
   "Night Work"

The Dickinson Review
   "The Great Blue"

Green Mountains Review
   "Christmas Morning"

Ironwood
   "Abel"
   "Cold Frame"

Kansas Quarterly
   "Bluefish Run, Machias, Maine"
   "Sunbath"

North American Review
   "Children"

Poetry
   "Rhodos"

Ploughshares
   "The Story"
   "Tragedy"

The Reaper
   "Cain"

Contents

I
The Hard Shapes of Paradise

Children

Light strives between the geese
steering through the leaf rafts,
arrives between the houses, up the drives,

hunts among the bare trees beyond town
where the buck browses, spent and restless.
Dowses the cedar swamp where does yard up.

When you and I were children, we wanted none.
Children sometimes do, rocking their dolls,
their nunlike selves in the shade of lilacs.

That hatchery in the Rockies? The mountains blazed,
hurting our eyes, everything so brilliant, so breathless.
Rainbow trout flashed, dimpled the concrete pools.

We felt like film exposed, thrilled and barren,
wondering at geese, up and down the flyway,
beating the thin, fissionable air.

They mate for life. I don't know why.
It is a sin not to shoot the pair.
Yet we insist and cling.

I like a shed, one dirty bulb, the privacy of woods.
You love a room with high, clear windows.
Don't you remember? How birth left you alone again?

And the little deaths of sex?
I cannot see by light that buries shade,
that cleaves and purifies, by hope

that radiates the schoolyard, shining on the chains,
bright as snow over coalfields in Pennsylvania.
Cape Cod is a silver hook I bypass into Maine,

to the end of the continent of light, where dusk
begins, where the yellow bus looms at 3 p.m.,
the shortest day, delivering children in the dark.

Feeding Time

for Linda McCarriston

They have no intentions
of learning, stamp the sod
because others feed them.

They breast the fence,
their eyes
the rich eyes of growing gods.

Who can blame them for being
what ignores us?
They are innocent as tyranny.

The adults tower,
flash the whites of their eyes
at small ones underfoot.

Looking down, they know their work,
back into the dark
evening which they are.

The Nature of Prayer

When the evening wind shifts offshore,
sifting in its small cool, the horses
gallop happily the length of the fence.
Clouds lour; the charged line ticks.

Noon drives them to shade like meat.
Flies follow in little confusions,
stains in air. The steers
drop to their knees, rock down,
monkish in the alders.
The mare and gelding stand in sleep,
head to tail like Molly and Leopold.
They switch each other's face.

Last week, a black, dripping moose,
its palmated rack festooned with kelp,
burgeoned up from the marsh,
strode through the hot wire without a shrug.
The animals watched.
The silver strand sprang back to the posts,
coils of light around the god.

At night they rut the dirt around the tub,
pock and shit the meadow, heads
down in darkness, as if their necks
were sore with worship. Raised, their eyes
gather stars like rivets in harness.

The Difference

The moon swells, so huge
barbed wire casts a perfect shadow.
The snow is cream.
I can't bring myself to cross,
ruin the pasture, my closed mind
parallel to things, leaning in.

Out there, the steaming beasts,
larger in this light, stand together,
like musk ox, mastodons,
as if the edges, shadows and sheds
threaten death . . .
as if they could
walk the line that holds them.

Easter 1946

Italians came out of the city in cush
black Buicks, parked by the gate
where the steers clumped or stood
in the middle of New Jersey.
They draped their coats on the rail,
argued like celibates, softly choosing,
then daintily side-stepped into the pasture,
herding in patent-leather shoes,
crooning to the lucky one.

Big, sweet as a nation, it permitted
an arm around its shoulder, the shiv
to slip into the jugular, twist,
slit so quickly
there was no gush or splatter.
The blood pulsed ordinarily,
soaking the brisket. The scene
a tapestry: peaceful men
watching a beast's last, amazed steps.

All the knives came out.
They worked in a ring, rolling back
the warm rug, undressing the purple flesh.
The stomach wallowed out. The saintly head,
finally alone in the grass, stared
past life, and the quarters, front and hind,
in shrouds, vanished, trunk lids
slamming like oak.
They folded the hide,

passed it to my father with the money
as if it were the flag.

Drawing on their black coats
over the immaculate shirts,
they passed a wickered bottle.
Peace had just been signed in the Pacific.
I commit myself
to the fine hands of Italians.

Opening Day

You kill the engine,
shift to reverse, soothe out the clutch
and sit back to take in the fringe of spruce,
the laureled edge of blueberry barren
where argument stops.

On the southwest branches
dew catches fire. In the rear mirror
clouds smoulder along the horizon
like piles of contagious sackcloth.
You tap a beer for the angel

that usually emerges,
among your tall, wandering notions
steps gingerly into the open,
browses the final green, blows steam,
stamps a coal, imperial hoof and blindly

looks west into the remnant, ragged aura
you are snug in, downwind, glory
it has hidden from since dawn.

Each year you gut one, sauté the liver,
essence you've lugged home in a plastic sack.
The rest, caped and split, cut and wrapped.
Gods know enough to eat
something wild once in a while.

The loaded rifle in the cab is oil-rubbed,
true-cross and blued bone.
When the angel steps forward,
quivering with intuition,
last light gilds the front sight,
guides the lead eye east. The animal drops,
quaking as if the sun went off.

Spent, it winters in the humming
crystals of your brain.
Thawed, it's soft as women
even women eat.

Vestigial

The *Dolphin* shudders out from P-town,
out the vein between the ochre dunes,
in dull rain merges with the sea, begins to roll.

A voice from the pilot house
tells about the mammals, as if they were stars.
We'll all be back by dark.

Some are eating the expensive dogs. In salt air
we smell the mustard. Some are leaving their spume
riding the wake. Some get up a joy:

a mountain of flesh will heave for us,
bring the bottom up, empty us and sound
our single fathom.

As if on cue, a long, black freight,
for what seems a minute parallel, but distant,
trails itself, spouts, dives.

"Finback," says the voice, disappointed. Already
we discriminate. The ship drums and staggers.
We look to one another. Nothing rises in the heart.

Of all things, this is what to fear, the rolling
steel sea, terns and gulls that wheel,
screech above the leavings.

But what you love finally breeches:
gray, riven, patched with mortar, the humpback
lifts a battered fluke, waving you in.

You rise on your toes, squealing with the rest,
see the one low eye focused on you. It blows.
Sprayed, you know you breathe the same air.

Back on the swaying pier, your legs vestigial,
you want to go down on your belly.
Your tiny eyes swim among the beached cars.

The Great Blue

The heron catches my eye like a dace,
a sliver of herring. It sees
invisible shrimp in a tidal pool,
mosquito fish the color of mud,
small green crabs in the green hair.

The ocean rolls out pewter.
Rollers, rising out of Fundy, over the Banks,
start the nuclear roar, strew
flayed kelp along the beach.
Stainless light scours the granite knees.

The heron glides, flaps, glides
to a blasted spruce, collects itself like an umbrella,
spews back a chalky stream onto the scrubbed rocks.
It sheathes itself beneath a wing,
shuts its brazed eyes.
Lifts one leg.

The sliding sea shifts the junk around:
gray boards, half-skinned cedar poles
jamming in and out. An orange crate
tips and wallows; nests of rope and wrack
writhe on the grit. What's left.

At low tide,
at the edge, at the end,
the bird steps, slowly on the seared
purple plane. It cocks its head,

an overhead pick, its eye
a slip of original light

that Polwart probably noticed in an evening sky,
in 1601, or livening a Flemish painting,
or in the streak in a Bosch fish-belly.
So fresh. He wrote:

   "The crane must aye
   Take nine steps ere she flie."

Nine?

To fly, the heron simply leaps, lifts, wheeling
over its own broken cloaks
that take shape in flight, hunch
through this new light doming the metal sea,
light cleaved nine times. Nine.

Circuitry

Stapling wire under the barn
drawing the juice from one place to another,
I fell apart . . . flat on my back on the damp ground.
Sunless, strewn, sudden as stroke,
or sanity.

The pliers were too heavy to lift.
The 12/2 Romex a frozen snake.
I stared at the junction box, a small hotel,
at the copper tips, the gay
plastic wire-nuts.

I heard, inland, the diesels
whine through their gears like amplified
nightcrawlers, skewering the soil beneath my skull.
The gray leads dangled like roots, as if I'd
torn the building from the earth
and finally rested.

Before the war,
when drifts were deep and ice
sheathed the line to town and back,
breaking it, some of us would run from pole to pole,
find the gap, then stand there, taking turns,
holding the ends, feeling for a voice
to pass on through, down to the point
where houses cluster like shoes.
I lied I'd overheard
an answer climb the hill
to the tiny, varnished office by the dam.

16

Night Work

It's crazy to split wood
under the wide moon.
Sleepless, taller on the snow,
the arc of his ax almost wild,
the mute works beside me.
Each bolt halves, quarters,
grain shining open.

He drops his ax too,
wanders into the field
bathed with icy, lilac rags.
We might be up there,
floating on the rocks and pumice.
He knows the gravity,
light as he is.

Fox tracks wind like a knotted rope.
It barks to call its other. The crystal
echo freezes the changeling hare,
that silhouette growing into ghost.
White, it might survive its disappearance.

I doubt it. Shadows recede like hair,
the starched nurse rising.
The snowy owl sits in the birch;
there will be tufts, enameled bone,
rubies in the sugar.
Tall, dark and handsome, on his knees,
understands, her pocked face glaring down.

I go with the dwarf
through the gate into the garden,
healed over: parsnip knuckles,
glazed cabbage heads, bronzed chard
cast in romance not like sleep's at all,
that old poultice.
We are not supple enough
to cinch such wonderful configurations,
knots, tourniquets
we can shake open loose to dream.

Her stare at zenith
returns us to ourselves.
No one goes his own way. Whole,
we may as well work.
The ax handle is an honest bone, clapper
tolling in the cold metacarpals, up
the ulnae, radii, across
the balcony of clavicles,
summoning the entire hospital staff.

Bringing in the Light

Grapes, faded, heart-shaped leaves, vines,
a harmless, classical frieze
grays on the wall the way Pompeiian lovers hold
in ash, not to seed the world
until the mountain shifts its thought.
Motes, like white cells,
wander room to room in fossil drafts,
dull the parlor organ, grim settee,
the oil lamps that used to seethe.

The feral corners of this house
cloud the mind that goes against itself:
trenches the lawn, buries the Romex,
probes the cellar stones and snakes it in,
new synapse to a socket.
Then inserts the switchbox in a shallow grave
chiseled in the bone-thick, horsehair plaster,
wallpaper pasted with the rat-chewed brush
Mary Munson left in the attic when Alva was a boy.

I flip it ON. Lymph swells, hums,
drawn from the recent, carboniferous dead,
surges toward the kitchen where the soft-white bulb
distends, mind itself turning things to salt
because it looked ahead.
I'll blaze the lawn, draw moths,
death's-heads, drive the beasts
back beneath the trees, infect the stars,
read at night
new books that expose and forgive me.

Waiting for the Water to Fall

Men walk out so calmly,
blown snow swiping their tracks.
Whole parties vanish in the glare,
the white-out that fillets the trees,
scales shadows back,
holds up the bleached bone.

I wait in my chair
swiveled to an inner wall
where nothing is especially hard,
deep, or clear, when I have iced
nothing and can tolerate prediction:
early swallows with their blued swoop,
ducks, just up from the south,
that dip and gabble
in the swelling rug of algaebloom.

Then sunset lays the shadow of my cottage
into shallows. Bluegills appear,
fin above their swept nests,
steer, stop, start . . . perpendicularly
suspicious. A crayfish, backing down,
derelict, clouds itself in the exhausted silt.
A clam trail ends without a clam.

And then the bass surges through,
a revivalist to see the children,
waving its avuncular tail,
trailed by an old catholic pickerel

who swallows argument whole,
whose long, eclectic stomach
dissolves the case of what's missing,
gives me back
the little name of everything.

Then shadow generalizes.
The last thing I see is a pair of eyes,
on stalks, that have also decided not to move,
but wait for other weather, a hot,
dry dynasty with fire-storms,
baking a desert fringe around the lake,
drawing the big fish off,
down among their own, in deep
conversation and pharaonic dark.

Running with Dogs

Under the evergreens I slow down,
sidestep tiny orange trees, chanterelle
burgeoning in shade, their spores
apocryphal, released from ice, maybe
filtered here from stars.

My dogs find bones, one of their kind.
Sniff without grief. The long teeth
are loose in the gray, porous jaws
bedded in moss. Shot for ripping the kids' goat.
The father raged in the yard for love.

Running like this is a viney thing to do,
in and out of incredible light
that waters my eyes, blurs a stone wall,
halos and overexposes the clean, broken
lines of their house, heats the aura
around his settled cars, hub deep in soil,
above their back field graves,
the hard shapes of paradise.

It's been years since I left Hawaii, since
the Christmas Island blast.
Milk-green light infused Honolulu,
rising, bloody in the upper air.
We cried with the others by their cars
parked over Punchbowl Cemetery,
the birds singing at midnight.

The dogs swing back into the woods,
off the sunlit blueberry barrens of Maine,
trot and sniff in shadow where the chanterelle
burst upon the eye and I walk, wanting to drop
to my knees beneath usual spruce.

Clam

The sand seethes on the ebb
that hates to go down.
I want a big one, jammed
deep in the blue clay,
impressed by my footstep
that sends up its geyser.

Some men do this for a living;
that's the problem with living.
Bent, groins in torsion, they rake pecks,
bushels. I'm only looking for one,
a Viking ship, perfectly preserved.

I dig with my fingers. Grit
packs in under my nails; a little blood
pinks the seepage when I stroke
its broken china beak.
I pinch the tip, rock the animal

until it spits and gives.
Soft-shell, I mustn't crack
or hurry this. Shock-white,
it comes, tight between the praying valves,
big as my fist.

Knee-deep in the paralysis of Fundy
I rinse and polish it,
heavy as a puppy in a woman's palms.
It's its own fault.

Back on the hot sand, I sever the sweetmeats.
It sighs open, tired of men.

There's the yellow band,
black-capped neck, mouth/foot like a chewed
nipple. The stomach is round as my Waltham,
foul gray as the word "globular."
I ring the mass with my knife,
toss away the siphon, stare at the mess

and, yes,
tip it into my dry, unanticipating mouth,
bite the pod, chew the surgical tubing,
taste fifty million years of saline,
iodinic flowers cold as mind.
I swallow it pretty much whole.

Offshore

Men haven't been up enough to laugh,
mouths still sour with sleep, okolehau.
The rainy side of the Molokai slopes
begins to steam. The boy rows out,
drops his roped stone, takes one look landward,
spits in his mask and falls over backward
into the sea.

His body, his mind, cool with alarm,
pull downward, hand over hand,
the stone already moored, calmly in its own
muffled explosion of sand. What he left
ashore, apocryphal.

Beneath an overhang of iridescent coral,
his spine arches happily as morning
spears the fissures, and a squirrel-eye,
a grouper, among the menini and wrasse,
turn and mill on each last bit of one another.
He's down so long, drawn to shadows,
shapes that stare, half-lit, his mind
begins to drift. Food for thought.

The skiff overhead thunks against the small waves
breaking on the reef. It bobs, *trompe l'oeil*,
illusory as air dying inside, fuddling. So,
he rises, of course . . . and on the beach,
in shacks, the drinkers and sleepers
kick at their sheets, to launch themselves,
to surface without dream.

Fluid

for Bon Gordon

A brother with a head as heavy
as that, born so, worries like a lake,
too calm, winter or summer, a medium
half oil by now, so close to people.

He has more space to carry
what your eye fills with
at sunset, because it is impossible
for anyone to deal with vermillion,
patches of brassy sunfish
waving their transparent tails in sandy coves,
shifting the crystals, hollowing the nests
that catch paradisaical clouds,
eggs and milt sifting down.
Overhead, the spent, wide-eyed angels
fin, nervous as traffic.

He is a medium, too, like Louvia Leferrier,
twelve, bird-voiced, in Vermont,
who found lost cows without leaving the kitchen,
bunches of keys "near a stream of light,
by stones," she told me. People
called from Alaska to ask the different girl.
He tells you your future.

What to do . . . auras of eggs and milt
confuse and blear, make you
see through, not see
aquariums of DNA. You think you've gone crazy,
but that's not so. Chromosomes

steer and switch through the tropical gouache
of their own stirring, through coral lobes,
iridescent brains, the door of a pastel castle.
If you do not shake it, it's calm in there.

In the stairwell of your house
the patches of bare plaster are cracked,
unnamed rivers, trails, arroyos.
There are leaves of faded wallpaper,
layers, packets that will not steam and peel,
cheeks of smooth old Russian mothers
who laugh to hear little sister think so much,
who say why worry much about a brother who,
back and forth in his bowl,
keeps you after all.

A home is a castle. In yours
the stairs are too steep for him to climb
balancing his burden, not without
your easy dog, big as Africa,
who stands by his side, keeps pace,
like a woman with a jug on her head,
who doesn't spill a drop,
animal that takes us all
up and down Olduvai,
across the geology of thought,
through the hydraulics of origin,
our hands wrapped in its thick
salty collar.

Bluefish Run, Machias, Maine

As if the banks were lined by spiders
tossing long, shimmering filaments
the river crawls along like prey.
I've come, parked with the rest,
all our radios on to the local station
for news of ourselves, in between the music
hard people are soft on. Cut-bait, treble-hook plugs,
wobbling spoons, plop among the frantic menhaden.

Cars jam the A&P lot, the store so empty
Fred and the butcher stand in their aprons,
arms folded in the big glass doors.
The Georgia Pacific, humped with pulp logs,
pulls up at the crossing, diesels wheezing,
drumming while men climb up
to see from the piles.
There is a flush of small fish, as if a wind
frittered the surface, or someone
blasted it with birdshot.
Then another.

They wheel the old folks down from the manor.
They sit in a row like dental work. No kids in school
but here with their battered rods, freshly taped.
Teachers are seen, pushing off in their skiffs.
Big hats down over their eyes. Someone says
the postmaster is having a fit,
who won the Six Mile Lake Fishing Derby twice.

A reporter goes from elder to elder.
Not one of them remembers anything like it,
bluefish down from the west, chasing "pogies"
clear under the falls in a thrash of blood,
under the stilted balcony of Helen's Restaurant.

Next morning the river has died, badly bitten.
Gulls wander overhead.
Blown with trash, the banks recede like gums.
Skiffs are hauled, turned over,
shells the crabs eat out.
Over coffee at Mac's, people count.
Some have caught a fish. Four crescent tails
are nailed to my woodshed door.
For summers to come
they will draw the iridescent flies.

Rhodos

The bay where god sank dreams.
Apollo astride the harbor, Colossus,
feet as long as barges planted on the pincer jetties.
Priests hum, agents whistle, everyone here has
taken a dive to rummage in the coral,
dun as eels sinuating the reef
that like paradise was lightly salted jewels
when gaff-rigged shadows
plied beneath the lustrous groin.

Above the beach, sand-pink, the Hotel del Rosas,
chancred with bougainvillea. Black suits, white shirts
click their heels by your table.
Up the cliff, the fortress of St. John
leans, re-frescoed by Il Duce, whose peasants in arms
look like him: Giotto da Capone.
The snarl of lawnmowers rips the air
dressing the sandstone acropolis, the arena.
Scissors flash where crones crop the Moslem tombs.
Seaward, over the golden onion dome,
three American destroyers
swim on their chains
while whores in the doorway of The Kit Kat
watch the M-boats work between the stone jaws.

Who would not
sail around under the imaginary,
given a sequestered bay, just live a little
on small fish laid out like keys on an oval salver,
some greens, soft cheese, an opulent lemon

next to a glass of rose wine,
light as the monastery bells
wafting from Lindos where the monks
still inch up and down the towering walls
pulleyed in a basket by an old gray donkey?
Just sit by the shop selling goatskin boots
carved with their own hands, now free for talk,
to watch the sun
stretch the shadow of the god toward Turkey?

He is down there now, trenched.
Morays anchor in his pores, strike at passing fish,
bright as glass eyes, as lipstick, the kelp
camouflaged varieties of human skin.
A signalman from Maine shakes out the evening flags,
imagines the giant guarding the port.
He is in love with one of the girls.
She can't go. The old story:

that night he drinks off limits in the Walled City,
yanks the veil from a woman
whose husband and brothers cut off his balls,
sew them in his mouth and slip him,
gagging, from the pier.

Waiters, fishing from the quay, haul the body.
The warships leave. The bars
roll down their corrugated iron doors.
The overnight steamer from Piraeus,
babbling, swells in the harbor,
churns the surface.

Blades

An eight-inch, double-edged Arab dagger
with ivory and brass wrapped handle
to remember the Alhambrah. What did I do there
in another life, slit a little Visigoth?
Dump her bright body into the fishpond,
in the brass light by the flower bed
footing the long stair to the summer palace?

The Finnish *puuko* on my dresser has no hilt
to stop it, or my hand sliding out
on thin ice. Nana kept it of her husband's things,
Johann dead at forty-three, lungs full of quarry dust
and three years in an Estonian labor camp.
Her hooked fingers, bulbous knuckles,
peeled onions, nipped threads as she crocheted.

I purchased a broad, flat blade in Munich
with *für Hackenfleish* etched on one side,
saw-edge and caping tip, after the bus from Dachau.
My wife was pregnant; we strolled
the ditches of ash, nubs, and geraniums.
It lies, sheathed, in my green toolbox,
opens cans of paint.

I clean my nails with the tiger-striped
Camillus pocket number
bought in Franconia Hardware
the afternoon we buried our daughter.
I pare skin from a cold New Hampshire apple,

thin as the atmosphere,
the red breath of a child's planet.

Natural History

Under the giddy bulbs
strung on their poles like constellations,
under the frame and axle of the Ferris wheel,
bone by bolted bone dismantling,
the bluish cloud of a tent sighs down,
placental in the trashed field.

We carry our kids, obese with sleep,
not dreaming of what they have seen in the cages,
on the steel wire above the beaten ring.
The plywood booths fold into themselves.
Diesel semis rock and shiver beneath the beasts.
The children, tucked into the parked cars
are safe as freaks behind glass.
They won't remember our passing,
concerned faces peering in.

We sat in the bleachers like students.
We stand outside, gray and exhausted,
as if we were pegged.

A herd, in thunderous gloom,
circles for days and nights, sniffing,
trumpeting above the expired folds,
spans and ivory by which they remember.
Then they amble off.
Natural history is oxymoron.

Engines cough, roar in the lot.
Headlights clown, crazily into each other,
exposing us over and over.
Heaven has collapsed and we are the poor
stars again, blind and happy.
Our children will never run away.

II
Apocrypha

The Story

for Jerry Aidlin

Apocryphal, the sweet Hawaiians,
a few blue silk clouds
hooked on the shark-tooth Waianes,
root-smell and ginger
hanging in the rain forest,
Honolulu damp with flowers:
torchy African tulip, St. Thomas trees
like giant, sorry, missionary lilacs,
night-blooming cereus that have had their night,
shriveling at dawn . . . yellow sea anemone
a child collected and left on a lava-stone wall.
And hula girls too sleepy to wave their bodies,
arms draped with heavy leis
just for your arrival: tuberose, pikake,
star-jasmine, common orchids. Oahu
beginning to steam, a green chrysalis drying.

In Maine, Nana plucked at the victory garden
sluggishly: babushka, clumpy shoes, legs
wrapped in Ace bandages . . . all Europe
on her knees, and a neighbor's white rabbit
hopping in the brilliant lettuce.
CRACK . . . my father's black pistol,
the rabbit screaming,
hauling its hindquarters like an Easter glove.

I garden all summer, ruthlessly.

Because the good green book
doesn't say we can return. I am not

to be forgiven Paradise: women,
men, islands whose shapes console
no more than coral bits in sand.
I have to forgive my father
for anything said or done, as he did his
to be rid of gods . . . as good gods
forgive youth, as all
put Mother in the park.

A decent text. I tell how,
one moonlit night, in Halawa Valley,
I drank okolehau, smoked gold and tore apart,
ate with my fingers a huge, red Samoan crab,
netted in the pool below the falls.
Steamed it like the devil in banana leaves.
Squeezed the amber juice of liliquoi
all over the snowy flesh.
Then swam among the fallen blossoms:
plumeria, white and saffron, ginger petals,
outrageous hibiscus with their papery lips.
I had the whole place to myself.
So I made a little tii-leaf boat with orchid cargo,
set my soul afloat.
It was the last time I saw it.

It isn't the earth I want.
You don't want it either.
You like the story.

Observatory Hill, Manchester, New Hampshire

Before plastic, we heaved fifty-gallon drums,
galvanized pails, stood knee deep in the load,
rocking and rolling the raw leavings out.
We saw it all; we smelled it all.
Two alleys four blocks long filled a dump truck;
we were off, trailing clouds, to the living dunes
that seep into the river at Pinardville.

After work we bathed in the granite quarry
that drops off the east side of The Hill
sixty-five feet below that fieldstone tower
with its spiral stairs, Chinese, tin hat of a roof
shadowing the twin cannons like a sundial,
a wand that waves from south to north, each day
blessing the mounted binoculars, parking-lot chains
frozen in coats of municipal green. Blessing
the vast, concrete reservoir on top,
its chain-linked, obsidian water.

Astride my cannon over the city
I lean out, *trompe l'oeil.*
St. Mary's verdigris roofs
float above the steamy tenements
West across the chemical Merrimack
struggling by the mile of red
brick mills, now condos, offices,
quichedoms, and clinics.
This side of the river, the powder-blue pool
glitters in Derryfield Park, in sepia air,

and here and there a white truck crawls an alley,
hopper screaming, eating thousands of bags a day
that swell in the sauna like wives.
I smell the city's patina . . . saint's feet.

St. Joe's, East, under The Hill,
like the old man himself, withdraws,
just out of the aura at the back of the crèche.
Bill and I, each on a cannon, talked of him once,
how sexless as Mary, how that must be the point.
Water, babies, garbage in common.
No one prays to Joseph.

Bill is somewhere in the mills today
fitting and stapling carpet,
father of three on his knees.

The smell is in our pores. My mother
made us hang our clothes
to flap their sour wings on the tree
outside the cellar door.

He's gone religious. Like the Amoskeags,
the French Canadians, Doby the one-nut
short-stop, Jackie Kapopoulos the point guard
and Jesus, Bill says, "What I want
isn't here."

In a graveyard of cars, poked by raspberry canes,
a gray, floorshift Plymouth Six is still
rancid with us. We are the crazies
who one night climbed the ten-foot fence and,

against all law, dove into the city's
virginal font that pressures water all over town.

We have been in every tap and mouth.
We swam in moonlight beneath the tower
like rare, pink Amazonian porpoises,
with one glowing bar of Ivory soap.

The Invention of Handball

Airing in the yard,
the man squeezes a ball,
tosses it against the wall on impulse,
relieved to see something come back.
He has murdered his wife.
A thief steps in,
whacks it with his hand
to be rid of the evidence,
returning it to sender,
who doesn't want it anymore,
is desperate to be rid,
sick of squeezing
what really happened
from what happened.
And so on, pairs of men
step in to keep the ball in play
for other reasons.
Convicted, they learn to use
their left hands too, knuckles,
dream of a back wall, side walls,
high ceilings with embedded lights.

Farmer

Barned since birth, they stood in the seamy stalls
all winter beside the mountainous Jersey,
her loins ravined, stave-ribbed, udder
dragged and chewed. The sire they will never know
lies in isolated pasture, well enough disposed,
seed in the freezer.

In spring he towed out the two of them,
bawling at the landscape. They froze,
then slowly made their way all around
inside the barbed wire. Down by the sliding bank
they looked quite brave, chased each other,
all akimbo, slipping in their own shit, flat to knoll,
gate to shed and back again, panicked by their lungs,
the involuntary lunging. They grew
heavy and slow by fall.

Now look at their heads in the tub
like heavy boots that love each other,
eyes warped open to the sun. The stiff wind
wags their hides, brown and white maps,
draped on the rail.

He gave them names by which to kill them.
During the war he gave his son as easily,
thoughtless as he was. He can't bring them back.

Winter has driven the flies inside
to sleep by the billions. The two of them

nosed his proffered hand, palm of grain.
Even as he slaughtered them, their mother
freshened. As does his half-dark oath.

Fenced

I'm finished sweating this pasture,
framed now with steel mesh,
top strand barbed.

The sheep, the cattle,
let out of the barn, walk with their heads down,
make a first path all around
before they go for water.
The kids sit on the stile,
legs dangling, shining from their bath.

They say how *good.*
I remind them that animals wander into woods,
go over to the blueberry barren in the pesticide,
or gorge in the salt marsh on eelgrass
they can't digest . . . that sheep
find dogs to tear them.

Hopping down, they shake gold grain in tin pans.
As if they were begging.
The animals hear and obey.

I tell them they would chew the garden down.
Lambs in the road. Angry neighbors.
I tell them to shut the gate when I go out.

Click

The gelded appaloosa dozes,
head in the leaves of the apple tree.
Dong like a baby's leg.

I woke up hard this morning, numb,
bladder full. I relieved myself by the barn,
scooped his quart of fitting ration.

He whinnied and rolled a bloodshot eye,
picked up the white plastic pan with his teeth,
brought it to the gate as usual.

Yesterday, I tried to switch his pasture
to a paradise of green with a few sheep.
He chased the white ewe into the barbed wire.

Could he know his clod-flung will?
How sheep panic . . . freeze in your arms
to be shorn or bled?

Back in his worn lot he seems content.
The fence clicks, a pulse surrounding him,
cutting us off from one another.

If I shut the current down
he obeys the dull throb in his veins,
not knowing the difference,

how sex grafts wounds that otherwise
seal too quickly, heal like ice,
or one thought:

horsemen riding in
to get it all over with, on mares trained to hear,
in the dark between stars, one click.

Dead End

The river squeezes here
between two granite heads.
Once in a while one of us rows,
upstream, the current arcing us over.
To get the mail, the news,
or leave forever.

Strangers, driving down the road,
imagine a span, then gripe in disbelief,
as if we'd failed, the pretty, coastal town
settled on the other side. A few
stand on the bank, quiet in the shimmer,
watching the rip, the tide
moving in, lifting the outward flow,
or the flow collapsing on the ebb.

We have failed.
The river is cleaning itself.
The clams are good again.
Eelgrass is growing back,
greening the flats; tiny snails
glide the tough stems, so flounder
come in with the tide to feed,
with them the ducks.
And children row the shallows,
with pitchforks spear the sole
like brown hands on the mud.
No one is hungry.

We tell the disgruntled
that ten miles inland hangs a lovely
blue suspension, that many drive
back and forth, from one end to the other,
as stars do, shifting together
through the universe.

Word is, though,
the stars just started out.

Thaw

Rising languidly from the cedar swamp,
deer nose across the broken wall
weakened by winter.
In the field, each takes on the new light,
stripes, whipped there . . . buckles for an instant
then stands infused, radiant, looking up.

Across the pasture, smoke souls
slip from our brush fires. The breeze is low.
You can hear the gay snap of aristocratic limbs,
the alder marrow and birch sap fry.

They browse so nervously, looking about
to run back into the dark, having for the moment
tasted something green in last year's grass.
They are like the rescued survivors of a camp,

not ready yet for spring. No fawns.
Our fires swell, leave their centers,
crawl the hay. By summer the field will be perfect.
The flames fan, sneak beneath the boulders,
vaporize on icy loaves, sticks
still sepulchred in shade.

Husbandry

Lambs stare from under the ewes
banked in the back of the crapped truck.
My neck sweats in cold, spring fog.
You lean against the bin, still soft, humorous,
your boots mired. Childless, we could afford
to be less ruthless if we dared.

They frisk in the decomposing garden.
Ewes ring the red Ford as if it were their fresh
slaughtered ram, lick the fenders for the salt,
dabbing with their eyes shut.

I grab a wether, bind its front legs,
sit it on its haunches. It leans against my knees,
dazes. We wonder why they doze so.
Some vow, imprint . . . promise to obey?

You look away a moment.
It slips, a sheath upon its end,
bleeds freely in the straw.
Would I keep these skills
if I lived alone?

Or hunt? Track a vanishing trail
only to leave one? You trust my craft:
hunting in the rain
when leaves and crust forgive, when deer
confuse a footstep with a clot of snow
dropped from a cedar tip.

In the chill of the north porch, glassed in,
we hang the carcasses high, to season them,
dangling like pagan statuary, piously
lopped at the wrists, neck, knees,
the marble grapes knocked off, scattered.

Haleakala, Maui

for Galway Kinnell

Downslope into the crater,
into the ground mist seeping knee-high
infused with chilly light
shot from other stone we have walked upon,
breathing stone's ether.
The cinders, clinkers of ancient heats and scree
give beneath my feet, two miles above the Pacific,
closer to the moon, huge tonight,
a night-blooming cereus
bending to her lover for her one drink.

I touch and find no face. I am nobody, finally,
a leper ambling in the hollow,
in the burned-out groin of Pele
where moonlight gilds the rim,
glints off the silversword,
cacti that grow like angels only here, feeding on ash.
I come to life so slowly. My blood cools,
lucky to feel this once, the earth as it was.

Seven miles east, past Kaupo Gap,
cornered by the crater wall, *nene*, only forty left,
flap and honk at the moon. Ino, park ranger,
priestess in white rubber boots,
comes out of the shack to see, strokes the mule,
croons her own slack-key, sterile joy.
Like the gods of her people she is unselfish,
wants no children now.

Here is the live quiet
close by the river of stars, dammed in one
sweet, unholy light, in air
softer than infant breath.
As it was.

Alive this long I must go down.
But here, in this old garden, I may for the instant
love, as earth by moon, doting face all lit.
After bloom, pocked and simple.

Whale Wife

She wheezes and beeps in her sleep
swimming languidly beside her new husband
who is large, kind, and full of grace.
She's been to Maui again,
watched Lahaina Road for spouts, whooshing
spasms of the battered Lord,
for Him to surface barnacled and scarred.
She stood with the others on the pier,
virgins gone overboard for just one ride,
through bubble nets and whey,
through the crystalline blue,
wagged all over the Pacific by the Magnificent.

I'd like to transmogrify, be somebody,
return to water, feel the original swell
at one with the enormous babies,
the open-hearted songs that sound like blizzards
boomed beneath the polar caps
by mothers in the Marianas Trench.
Twice a week I do laps.

I think she still loves me, her mind submerged,
tucked against His surprisingly warm, riven flank,
the two of them sliding along, hymning,
Him vast and dimly noumenal
through galaxies of brit,
shrimp, His tiny eye ageless in the dark.

I know, under our quilt, that she
knows the beached weight collapses.

Cain

He was fat and strong as a harvest animal.
His nails packed with dirt, his toes
like black olives . . . as if he were
burying himself alive.

Mother watched, helped me shovel him under,
shed huge tears "to make him grow." Then loved me.
It was hard to resist. Garrulous Adam gawked.
"Is that dead?" he asked. We just didn't know,
hadn't seen anything like it before,
Adam in doubt.
It saved his life enough.

I have lived well since,
tolerating labor.
I have high ambitions; I envy the god
who killed my mother and father.
Who lives so graciously alone
in his white house.
Abel could never.

I cannot be shaken. My suits wait to be filled.
My shoes glint in the closet.

Yes, I have loved. She is very, very beautiful.
Though last night, after many promises,
she bore me a daughter.

Benediction

The girl offers her arm,
lopped at the wrist, hugs with the other
stone flowers to her breast,
stands vandalized above an old man's grave.
I searched the alders for her hand.

Hem deep in snow, she floats.
Across the yard, Jesus presides.
She gazes shyly down,
in spring her marble toes
frozen as his will to rise.
He might have asked her anything.
Streaks of rust warm her hair.

Her sister Grace, in Reykjavik,
was buried to the waist intact, in black
Puritanic ash. Children shoveled her out,
cleared the slope of drowned stones
above the steamy city.
I saw this in *National Geographic.*

She has no wings. No Charity,
we stand these dumb things above our bones.
We pray, saying the names
sandblasted into the morbid granite.

Let's just say her hand
warms beneath the jacket of a dismal boy
walking roadside in the headlights.

Cold Frame

All summer it pushed the bib leaves,
Boston red, a dozen emerging babies' heads.
Now the chocolate block lies dumped on the plot.
You want a temple.

Able in small ways, I feel a little
weary now and then, as if I see by light
shining in your skin all winter
what makes my heart sink with joy.
You say my hands are still beautiful.
So they seem, now you've spoken.
I hide them in the mulch.

Yesterday's thaw drew you out.
It might be spring.
We scuffled along in the flat, wet leaves,
the leftovers, like the old days.
You sat on the frame
rubbing your feet together.
Your feet drive me crazy.

God knows, all these years, keeping the grounds,
the few animals, I'm solo still.
I whitewash the statuary, the ladies and gents
meditating here and there, trim
the shrubs around them. I like
to work with my hands, that's all.
No pyramids. Just a few green peppers,
tomato, brussels sprouts . . . the lettuce.

See delicate Pharaoh, gilded and pretty,
sadly poking his leafy meal?

Tonight your cornerstone will freeze again,
moldered, rounded some.
I have to go right now,
take the cold frame to the shed,
flush and scour it,
hang it to dry.

Dowsing in Eden

Her palms are raw. The tight olive bark
twists from the bone. Her arms quake, face drawn
while the forked rod shivers, splayed
like a doe at the water hole, bowing
while lions cough.

Shifting from foot to foot, I keep watch,
trying to feel a grief in my hands,
anything to hang on to. Economically,
she triangulates the meadow, having crossed a vein.
I want to tag along, drive pegs, run string,
but this is magic, not science,
what she feels, life below, coursing.

I have tried her wishbone on the lawn.
Approached the well, supplicant, my arms limp.
She laughs. I lack the chemistry, maybe the desire,
happy to plant ornamentals, forget
everything that she'd dig up.
She works that stick as if to raise a child.

Pointing at the place, triumphant, she drops the rod,
sparing me, having visited her living
she strides into berries with her tin cup.

Abel

It is hard to think about me.
I am the one who hangs back, confused as leaves
blowing, who scuffles among the gulls on the pier,
or stands head down at the end of the bleachers
listening to the music on the loudspeaker,
and again next day in center field,
face to the gray sky.
Who, summer nights, after rain, when the kids are out
picking nightcrawlers, and the park is a randomly lit
airfield, wanders in the fringe of every flashlight beam,
watched by the one parent smoking in her car.

I probably am harmless. I think
that's what angers Cain. If I walk a dog
it brings me back. If I wander into the bar
I don't drink, but watch the video game
as if conversant with electrons. In my clothes
town folk recognize their skins.
Cain says I lack ambition, though I supervise
the sale of every shovel, the arrival of the Greyhound,
my blank face in every window.

I can't explain myself.
There are others similarly dull.
We don't say much, but watch the long dirt rows
turn green. I am half here.

Children, their bodies glistening,
dive and shoot and die
all over town. They leave me alone.
They could never be mine, though I wish
sometimes to touch one.

Christmas Morning

Earlier, the orange Cat, swiveling,
squealing on ice-choked tracks,
unearthed Eden: icebox door, galvanized
water tank, Chevy fender, mush sofa
that began to smoke. Exposed a gray bulb
left whole by isostasy
to boys with Xmas Daisies, .22's.

I touch my mother's hair
as I pass the spare room.
Her mind is warm. She moans,
the light still on inside: shadows
of packing crates, frozen sheets on the line,
mounds of vegetable matter, bottles, a tire
twisting on a rope, packages of duck,
rabbit, partridge and fish guts
wrapped in *The Union Leader.* Dogs
strewn among the deer bones in the yard.
My brother and I broke everything:
cars, windows, ice, girls,
friends, and faith, like wind.

In a moment she will rise, find me up,
on my third cup considering
birth in acid, amino tidal pools
soured into life by morning light.
She will make "real" coffee, walk around me
to see what happened.

Drafts, moving through her robe,
smell like peat.

The guard, in his tiny, heated shed,
says the fires never go out,
despite the new law, the suffocating fill.
They are as old as the dump, as the will
to be rid of the evidence.
Zero weather, the dozer find an ember.
The village stinks and coughs by noon,
thinks the earth bitter.

Ma, the man is shoving new earth
over the old. The blade skims, grumbling,
sleeping along in a dream of waste.

Bitten

Breaking from the fog-soaked hay
I drop the boy from my shoulders.
Summer guest, he dashes for the rocks,
stands in his red T-shirt
screaming at the Atlantic.
I ease myself on a bleached root.

I loved to fish . . . maybe
I was a little older, loving the particulars.
I waved a yellow cane,
cast upstream where the headwaters
drop calmly over a wattled dam,
throating the Machias seaward.
My worm rolled along the silt.
Glass eyes switched in their sockets.
Bone lips clapped.

He's like a gull, this kid, a crab
all over the beach, halfway up the cliff
blind to tiny strawberries in the shale.
I listen for the stones
clicking beneath the crib-high rollers.

I was in awe of my father's vacancies.
How he'd stare without focus,
sit on a pier, thinking in that other language
he finally refused
to teach us. There was a farm beyond the horizon,
in bronze fields by the Id Fiord. That's all.

Now the kid is heaving stones,
trying to make them skip.
The moored skiffs rub and clunk like family.
In the bell-jar water, brit twist,
flash, scattered by the tinker mackerel.
Gulls feign sleep on every post.
Out in the swell, Clorox bottles
wag above the wire traps that mark the eel run.
Fresh from the Sargasso,
a ghetto squirms in the holding tank.
My father's father pickled them.

I take up my rod, cast nothing
at something for a while.
I listened to my father's words
pipping the surface like wing tips.
He spoke in English. What I wanted was the patter,
consoling vocal motor just around the bend.

Unsteady in the grass along the bank,
he says the water's fast beneath the glaze,
the anealing heat, waves that distort the town across
as terror did those times
he dragged a skiff like a sled,
walked the ice to get a letter.
Again he tells how eelers, spearing in the marsh,
found her in the spring, her face like tallow,
black dress laced with ice.
They towed her in, hauled out his first love
he thought had slipped away, inland.
All he knew.

One summer day when I was twelve
my line stopped mid-channel,
stiffened into a bow. Stalled,
I thought of rocks, roots, a pulp log.
I sensed a subtler heft. Mother of fog?
Father of mud?
I put the rod down, handlined through the weeds,
swirling as if a fist had them by the stems,
twisting braids.
I imagined the drowned girl, how I
would love her back to life.

The leader stretched, knots cinched. Instead,
a narrow, conniving head, opal eyes,
surfaced. Nylon wrapped its gill slits.
Muscle as long as my leg, it writhed
within itself, no struggle I can speak of.

I beat that eel with a stick until it quivered.
Took the lower jaw
between my thumb and forefinger
the way you do a fish. It clamped without malice,
having those special jaws. I heaved it like my
goddamned melancholy. It raked away my nail,
left me bleeding in the shallows.
I obliterated the head. Hours later
the shattered meat leaped in the grass.

Epiphanies should shrink to metaphor.
How many grieve
confirmed by ruthlessness to joy?

Take that white horse, sleepwalking in the hay.
I'll give the kid a ride. He'll never forget.
The nail grew back perfectly.

My father and I do not try
to net what lets us go. Our mouths
fill with galactic fry, wriggling, transparent
alphabets that slip the mesh,
leave us convulsed and dry.
The kid scavenges the beach for rope and weeds,
pulls in the pulling surf at heavy bodies of kelp.

After Image

A boy through the ice of the millpond,
tipping the plates, my father vanishes,
Vinal Haven, 1921.
Never drawn upward to begin with,
he swims with the current,
dashes for a breather hole, his brain freezing,
then slips from under the creaky lid,
over the dam and rises up,
yelling in the spiculed, steaming stream.

Many children drown. Dragged under,
they push against the marble dome
as if to come into the world.
The water rapes their throats,
crushes their small, awed minds.

He says he has nothing to fear at 80.
Does slow, perfect laps in the heated pool.
I swim some in the summer pond,
hold my breath in the shallows.

What have the children been told
by men they look up to,
men in hard, black boots
who shatter the ice with red axes,
who drag and grapple
to get at the bundles
snug against the dams.

Sunbath

Sweating, I rolled over
naked on a boulder smooth as flesh.
My cock grew, innocent, against the heat of stone;
I let go . . . woke and opened an eye.

Another stone was born beside me, the stone's stone,
large as a small suitcase, a gray-green baby
hemisphere, ridged with little Himalayas.
I moved.

I leapt faster than a rake when someone
fat steps on the tines, though now it seems an eon,
a dawning so long the earth
shifted from jungle to glacier.
I leapt as if I'd fathered a horror.

It rocked, slow, perfect diesel, diamond mind.
I want to say how lovely that was, hauled out,
the new creature sunning with the old,
a lineage of synapses, despite the blood change.
Except, the chill still shrivels me.

Its scaled legs fold under like the Emperor's.
Its jaws hook. Eyes, garnets in a clammy cave.
I know I'm missing something, shaped by severance,

moved by any hard shape in water.
Mineral beast, it mocks me for pulling back,
for thinking the green-clad warden was God,

who took his time, blew the shell,
the bright meat, like flowers and shards
all over the bay.

Frostfish

Face down for hours on the ice
above a green hole
the size of the shadow of your head.
Frostfish teem like tinsel in the shaft.
You yank and drop the treble jig
until the barbs strike,
then unhook the flipping fish
as if they were hot.
They flop then stick with the others.
A line of them as long as the lake,
head to tail, wouldn't be enough.

Fished again from deep snow behind the ell
they quiver on the kitchen counter,
the way forearms of eel
jump in the spiced oil, until the heat
seals them for good.
The girls turn away,
knowing the importance
of signs.

Dad laughs. Mom takes up her knife,
in her dark, preparatory mood
drops the silver bits into a sack,
heavy with cornmeal.
She says we have enough,
should all be grateful.

You jig until the run stops
when March has grayed and rotted the ice.
Your mother is tired of you.
The girls have learned to laugh.
They've begun to bleed.
He smokes beneath the spring stars
turning in one long school above the roof.
You swear even the sack moved.

Tragedy

Pigs loom, grunting by the shed,
embarrass the decent farmer,
lathered in his bathroom window.

Dipped in pine-tarred water, at 158 degrees,
the bleached carcasses shave so easily,
bristles falling over the blade.

He was beaten once for tossing
diseased chickens into the pen
when he'd been told to bury them.

Pigs develop tastes. He can't watch one
crush a squash. Fed flesh,
they will drag a child from the rail.

Still, like his dog eyeing lambs by the fence,
they are God's creatures, cutouts colored,
folded correctly, standing on the oak table.

Stropping, he watches a robin,
such a good listener, fat, orange
hunter, towing up the infamous worm.

A man in Nebraska raises African nightcrawlers,
salts and dries them like jerky.
His children ate them on TV.

The grackle has the meanest eye,
amber in a blued-steel head. Took a whole
morning to toss a milk-snake high in the air,

over and over hammer it,
then fly the limp thing off
like a chartreuse necklace.

Was it that snakes eat eggs?
Or that warm blood hates the memory of cold
coursing sluggishly in volcanic fog?

Hawks love snakes, tear,
swallow the cold bits as if to keep
the saurian power. Probably the snake,

pulling itself like a mitten over a frog,
hates its own satanic obedience.
The way a farmer hates a high field,

truck load, fat silo, stuffed elevator.
The way gods hate their creations
he loves the horizon.

Usual ruler, he steers broad ellipses,
a constellation crooning forward, diesel aria
for what the mindless past was, the infuriating green.

He cuts himself, runs the styptic
pencil in the slit, enjoys the sting,
pats his face with alcohol.

He mows, that's all, as beasts browse,
trek the Serengeti,
into the hot, orange glow.

The blades chitter, scissoring
the steaming hay, wheat, oats.
Moles skither, nosing up the timber,

some bitten, tossed by the dog that follows him
trotting in the stubble,
quartering the swathes.

In cool, gloomy barns, before dawn,
westward all over the country,
others are starting their engines.

Some gather at noon,
chew slices of white bread, pressed ham.
Gulp bottled water.

Under the few trees along the road
the diesels churn and knock,
familiar, idling bodies.

October Morning

Our headbones are tuned
to the cellos of fall, tongues
awake, bitten by the new cider's
mild irony, nice as the Hohner C's
of geese, so high their V's evaporate.

At the edge of the golden tamaracks
a cheddar doe lifts her head
into the dawn of opening day.
So.

So the bee violins and sparrow piccolos,
the summer tympany are gone.
Bales sulk against each other in Mahler's barn:
the defeated team's rough fans
huddled in the draining stadium.
On the moss at the north base of birches
squads of honey mushroom brown and pout
while the sun skulks along the horizon,
trying to get up, its rosé wine
stuffed in a paper bag.

So love is just your nervous will
to have another body,
fruit to rot beside you.
You've had enough of wonder.

Remember, a month ago, that warm evening,
how, beyond the casement window,

the sky was a California brush fire
behind the oak, and a thousand
passionate monarchs fluttered up, in waves,
each a hallelujah
hung like a flare on a pinked leaf.
This is how they slept together
on their way to Mexico. Night
put those Chinese lanterns out.

I'm not this medieval all the time.
A female wink, condescending as weather,
says that summer babies are conceived in fall.
But what is not?
The field with doe is ravaged just for June,
harrowed, mowed . . . for June,
June Haver, June Allyson, June Havoc.

Look, despite the mystery, a foetus
bobs all winter in the dark,
a swollen, falling thing
that shows its polished side in the summer grass.
Underneath, the vain flesh stains and sours.

This *is* the season for love.
The scholar in his office of paradox,
who is a father, puts the pistol to his head.
He knows the night watchman will find him.
The orchestra believed in
is finally heroic, instruments
packed in the bear-shaped cases,
fish coffins. The swallows, the monarchs,
light up a dusty bell, while the street band
plays "La Paloma."

Under this morning's blue skim,
that makes a noun of our pond,
trout are stripped for sleep, have done
their dairy business in the gravel.

And high among the beech, gone bone,
bucks step solitary ways, composing
half-notes in the first inch of snow.
They have clashed, like cymbals.
They hear the echo, rifling the swamp,
down where the sowed does
have to make their winter yard.

Comedy

Swallows dive, loop,
pock the oiled lake.
Rings break into flame,
sunset slaughtering the pale rocks.

Tired, I step back into the gloomy shed,
look into the split yellow eyes
of the black ewe, scraping grain from my palm.
She makes me look away.

Halfway up Katahdin I stopped,
climbed back down. Enough diamond-back river,
velvet-antlered forest, indigo horizon.
Let others get closer to heaven.

Reflection makes the lake beautiful.
The comic swallows skim,
flutter up in clouds of bugs.
Under their mud bulbs beneath the eave
their knives flash, glamorize the shadows,

then fold when the stars gang,
too little to hunger for
in that leather black,
spot-soldered celestial grit.

Fathoms

The filament, sinker, hook, and creature
sink away.
It hardly seems like fishing.
Me and a pressed meat sandwich in a tin skiff.

In shallows, the yellow reeds shiver. Some
thing thrashes once and heavy.
Or a wake V's the slick without visible cause.
Fact: a pickerel slash-grabbed a frog.
A smallmouth engulfed a moth.
Whole animals get used up, and water
returns to calm.

Fathoms down, in tannic gloom,
black fists, spot-lit hearts with lesions
loom in lime tubes. Bract maws.
Peat clods with marmalade legs.
Glycerin pallets. White-spiked smear lapels.
Processional elephant fogs.
Fungus bonnets in pneumonic orchestra.
It is the day after nothing.

The surface is calm.
A milkweed seed overhead
drifts, a little man under a parachute
headed upriver on a rumor. Far inland,
beneath a lidless sky, there is a bottomless lake
where generations form,
sluice into the river and down like friends.

There will be ten million years of peace
before they speak.

Now I have a twist of lilies in my throat.
I reel in and it takes forever.
There's my sinker, the bare Eagle Claw hook.
Maybe I won't go home this time.
It is the day before love.